Seasons

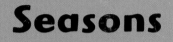

Fall

Patricia Whitehouse

Heinemann Library

Chicago, Illinois

Customer Service 888-454-2279
Visit our website at www.heinemannlibrary.com

Designed by Sue Emerson, Heinemann Library
Printed and bound in China by South China Printing Company
07 06 05
10 9 8 7 6 5 4 3 2

Library of Congress Cataloging-in-Publication Data
Whitehouse, Patricia, 1958–
    Fall / Patricia Whitehouse.
      v. cm. — (Seasons)
Includes index.
Contents: What are seasons?—What is the weather like in fall?—What do you wear in fall?—What can you see in fall?—What can you smell in fall?—What can you hear in fall?—What can you taste in fall?—What special things do you do in fall?
    ISBN: 1-58810-892-9 (HC), 1-40340-536-0 (Pbk.)
    1. Autumn—Juvenile literature. [1. Autumn.] I. Title. II. Seasons
(Heinemann Library)
    QB637.7 .W48 2003
    508.2—dc21

                          2002001162

Acknowledgments
The author and publishers are grateful to the following for permission to reproduce copyright material:
pp. 4, 5 J. A. Kraulis/Masterfile; p. 6 Michael Melford/The Image Bank/Getty Images; p. 7 Richard Pasley/Stock Boston; p. 8 Ariel Skelley/Corbis Stock Market; p. 9 Peter Correz/Stone/Getty Images; p. 10 Mark E. Gibson/Visuals Unlimited; p. 11 Peter Haigh/Alamy; p. 12L Jeff Greenberg/Visuals Unlimited; p. 12R Brock May/Photo Researchers, Inc.; p. 13L John Gerlach/Visuals Unlimited; p. 13R Ned Therrien/Visuals Unlimited; p. 14L Philip Gould/Corbis; p. 14R Warren Stone/Visuals Unlimited; p. 15L Ryan McVay/PhotoDisc; p. 15R Brian Hagiwara/Foodpix; p. 16L David Ponton/FPG International/Getty Images; p. 16R DigitalVision/PictureQuest; p. 17L Eyewire Collection; p. 17R Bob Winsett/Index Stock Imagery, Inc.; p. 18L Charles Thatcher/Stone/Getty Images; p. 18R Greg Beck/Fraser Photo; p. 19 Bob Daemmrich/Stock Boston; p. 20L Doug Mazell/Index Stock Imagery, Inc.; p. 20R Jose Luis Pelaez Inc./Corbis Stock Market; p. 21L C Squared Studios/PhotoDisc; p. 21R Darrell Gulin/The Image Bank; p. 22 (row 1, L-R) DigitalVision/PictureQuest, Yellow Dog Productions/The Image Bank; p. 22 (row 2, L-R) Kent Dufault/Index Stock Imagery, Inc./PictureQuest, Ned Therrien/Visuals Unlimited; p. 22 (row 3, L-R) Brock May/Photo Researchers, Inc., Robert W. Domm/Visuals Unlimited; p. 23 (row 1, L-R) Greg Beck/Fraser Photo, Peter Haigh/Alamy; p. 23 (row 2, L-R) Bob Winsett/Index Stock Imagery, Inc., David Ponton/FPG International/Getty Images; p. 23 (row 3, L-R) Warren Stone/Visuals Unlimited, Brock May/Photo Researchers, Inc.

Cover photograph by Ariel Skelley/Corbis Stock Market
Photo research by Scott Braut

Special thanks to our advisory panel for their help in the preparation of this book:

Eileen Day, Preschool Teacher
Chicago, IL

Ellen Dolmetsch, MLS
Wilmington, DE

Kathleen Gilbert,
Second Grade Teacher
Austin, TX

Sandra Gilbert,
Library Media Specialist
Houston, TX

Angela Leeper,
Educational Consultant
North Carolina Department
of Public Instruction

Raleigh, NC

Pam McDonald,
Reading Teacher
Winter Springs, FL

Melinda Murphy,
Library Media Specialist
Houston, TX

Some words are shown in bold, **like this.**
You can find them in the picture glossary on page 23.

Contents

What Is Fall?

fall

winter

Fall is a season.

There are four seasons in a year.

spring

summer

In most places, each season brings new things to see and do.

What Is the Weather Like in Fall?

Fall is a changing season.

Weather changes from warm to cold.

Some fall days are bright and sunny.

Other fall days are rainy and cold.

What Do You Wear in Fall?

On warm fall days, you can play outside.

You don't need a jacket or a sweater.

On cold fall days, you might need
a coat or hat.

What Can You Feel in Fall?

You can feel scratchy, dry leaves.

You can feel **frost** on plants.

You can feel a chill in the air.

What Can You See in Fall?

You can see pumpkins in a field.

You can see apples in an **orchard**.

You can see the leaves on trees changing colors.

You can see squirrels looking for nuts.

What Can You Smell in Fall?

You can smell leaves burning.

You can smell smoke from chimneys.

You can smell pumpkin pie.

You can smell other fall foods, like caramel apples.

What Can You Hear in Fall?

You can hear **geese** honk as they fly away.

You can hear leaves crunching under your feet.

You can hear people cheering at football games.

You can hear a **bonfire** crackle.

What Can You Taste in Fall?

You can taste crunchy apples.

You can taste sweet **apple cider**.

You can taste special fall treats.

This roast turkey is a special
fall food.

What Special Things Can You Do in Fall?

You can plant trees.

You can carve pumpkins.

You can celebrate special fall holidays.

Halloween and Thanksgiving are fall holidays.

Quiz

What are some things you see in the fall?

Picture Glossary

 **apple cider**
page 18

 **frost**
page 11

 **bonfire**
page 17

 **goose**
(more than one
are geese)
page 16

 **chimney**
page 14

 **orchard**
page 12

Note to Parents and Teachers

Reading for information is an important part of a child's literacy development. Learning begins with a question about something. Help children think of themselves as investigators and researchers by encouraging their questions about the world around them. Each chapter in this book begins with a question. Read the question together. Look at the pictures. Talk about what you think the answer might be. Then read the text to find out if your predictions were correct. Think of other questions you could ask about the topic, and discuss where you might find the answers. Assist children in using the picture glossary and the index to practice new vocabulary and research skills.

Index